Landmark
Essays

VOLUME 1

Landmark
Essays

VOLUME 1

Nancy Zapolski, Ph.D.
Joe DiMaggio, M.D.

LandmarkEducation

Landmark Essays, Volume 1

Copyright ©2008 by Landmark Education

ALL RIGHTS RESERVED

Published by
Landmark Education
353 Sacramento St., Ste. 200
San Francisco, CA 94111

ISBN 978-0-9821605-0-3

Printed in the United States of America

First Edition

To Landmark Education graduates everywhere.

Table of Contents

A Note from the Authors

When something moves us, transforms us, makes us feel and think in a new way, it might be considered a measure of greatness. Landmark Education and its programs have that kind of greatness. Landmark's technology is designed to provide a shift in perspective, an expanded view of what's possible and available to us in being human. This shift is achieved, in part, by presenting a tapestry of linguistic distinctions and terminology that enriches and transforms the way we inquire into *the nature of being human.* These distinctions allow for greater access to dimensions of ourselves, and our engagement with others, that we may not have fully explored before.

Landmark's technology is based on a body of work originally developed and created by Werner Erhard, a leading-edge thinker widely regarded for the unique and lasting contribution that his ideas have made in peoples' lives and in organizations around the world. His original work provided the foundation on which Landmark stands today.

This book, a collection of articles that first appeared in Landmark Education's quarterly newsletter, explores some of the tenets and principles underlying Landmark Education's technology. It points out what is possible if we step outside of what we know, and recognize and embrace our capacity to bring forth an entirely new possibility for living–not because it is better, but simply because that is what human beings can do.

These essays are not a written version of Landmark's flagship program, The Landmark Forum, which is a living and breathing event that occurs in community and cannot be put into writing. Rather, the essays point to some of the *distinctions* and *inquiries* addressed in that program in a way that is uniquely powerful and transformative.

–Nancy Zapolski, Ph.D. and
Joe DiMaggio, M.D.

Landmark Essay 1

If I Weren't My Past, Who Would I Be?

Nancy Zapolski, Ph.D.

Trying to change the past is pointless. Getting clarity about its enormous influence–positive and negative–isn't. Philip Roth, a novelist read the world over, gets to the heart of it in this passage on relationships:

> What had happened? Nothing particularly original. We had a fight, our first, nothing more or less annihilating than that. What had overcharged the rhetoric and ignited the resentment was of course her role of mother's daughter rubbing against mine of father's son–our first fight hadn't even been ours. But then the battle initially rocking most [relationships] is usu-

ally just that—fought by surrogates for real antago-
nists whose conflict is never rooted in the here and
now but sometimes originates so far back that all
that remains of the grandparents' values are the [cou-
ple's] ugly words. Virginal they may wish to be, but
the worm in the dream is always the past, that
impediment to all renewal.[1]

Trying to resist, change, or avoid the enormous influence of the past keeps us foolishly focused on it. Yet
we're reluctant to leave it behind, reluctant to transform the pervasive hold it has on our present-time lives.
Not doing so, however, results in an endless continuum
of living a "now" that is littered with the detritus of
the past. There's no better arena to watch this play out
than in our relationships.

When Tom and I were first married we had fights.
In my family, growing up, we considered fighting normal, healthy, and, I'm embarrassed to say, even
enjoyable. Every time Tom and I would even get close
to the possibility of a fight, however, he would politely
disengage and simply walk away. I didn't really understand it at first. To me, fighting and arguing was a way
to engage and work stuff out with the people you cared
about—I had seen it work time and again. It had passion, heat, drama—I considered it a special part of my
Italian heritage. Tom thought fighting meant something
was wrong—it implied conflict and upset. He had been

brought up in a family in which fighting was thought to be impolite, and just wasn't done.

If you take the area of relationships–a place (if you can call it that) we all spend a lot of time–the phenomenon of temporality (past, present, and future) becomes pivotal to how things play out. When we're in a relationship with others, in addition to bringing whatever *past* we have into the relationship, there is also a built-in, inherent, and implied *future* orientation. Because of this future orientation–especially when it's something like a marriage or beginning a new business partnership where you know you're committing to something for a long, long time–there is an added pressure to have things work out.

Imagine for a moment there are four different ways we might relate to the future: a *hoped-for* future (one in which we might wish it wouldn't rain so much in the winter months, or one in which we'd win the lottery, let's say), an *inevitable* future (getting older–it's unavoidable), a *planned-for* future (perhaps adding to our savings, or putting our kids through college), and lastly a *probable-almost-certain* future (one that is almost certainly for sure going to be what actually happens).

Each of these four types of futures has a different degree of influence. A hoped-for future likely won't impact us very powerfully, while a planned-for one may provide focus and momentum, but not necessarily a lot of power. The one that does have power and potency is the probable-almost-certain future, because it is in fact the one that is almost certainly going to be the way things turn out.

If we're straight with ourselves, our probable-almost-certain future is likely already pretty clear to us—we already see it happening. And let's say that future doesn't quite match up to the one we wanted. When we get glimpses of this or any future that is unwanted, our first response might be to say something like, "Oh well, even though things didn't quite turn out like I thought they would" (or are a bit troublesome and frustrating), "I'm really OK with it." After all, we think, other areas in our lives are working, so we can just let this one go. We don't really have to fix or change anything. It'll all balance out. However, when we settle things in our minds that way, or make those kinds of accommodations, there is no real possibility—we've essentially signed on to an unwanted future.

It's a temporality issue. À la Philip Roth's "worm in the dream," our past experience seems to be what's calling the shots. Here's how it works: When we have a bad day, or a bad experience, we put that past experience into our "future," as something we fear *will* happen again at some point, and something we want to make sure *doesn't* happen again. Or if we have had an exceedingly good day and something we did worked well, we store that past experience in the future too, hoping to recreate it as closely as possible. So essentially, we take our experiences and circumstances, which are behind us, and put our decisions about them—how we feel and think about them—in front of us. In doing so, we lock ourselves into relating to the past like it's going to happen again in the future. That's the wiring.

When we recognize and can *be* with our probable-almost-certain future (not change it, fix it, succumb to it, but be responsible for it), it starts to open up a space in which we can both complete something and invent something. (Completing the past is enormously powerful in and of itself—another point for another article.) Tom and I both laugh now about our respective pasts—instead of being an issue, they are deeply enriching to us. If we take out of our future everything from the past that we inadvertently placed there, and put it back in the past, then what's in the future is *nothing*. *Nothing* like a "clearing"—one in which we can be fully ourselves. It is from *nothing* that a *created future* can come into the picture. If we're going to create a future—in our relationships, in our work, in our lives—it's a matter of *saying so*. It doesn't rest on anything—it rests on *nothing*. And that's the foundation for possibility. In creating *possibility*, we get to know what's possible in being human.

Landmark Essay 2

A Transformative Encounter with Nothing

JOE DIMAGGIO, M.D.

Chinese philosophers hundreds of years ago said, *nothing is written.* Canadian author Margaret Atwood contemporizes that notion in one of her books:

> From an early age I knew my ambition was to be in a plot. Or several plots–I thought of it as a career. But no plots came my way. You have to apply for them, a friend of mine told me. He'd been around, so I took his advice and went down to the plot factory. Like everything else, there was an interview. So, said the youngish bored man behind the desk, you think you've got what it takes to be in a plot.

What sort of character did you have in mind? You could be the best friend. Or you could be the next-door neighbor, drop by for friendly chats. Or you could be some guy with lore—sort of like a coach. Teach the main character how to slice off heads, one-handed, with a sword. We can always use those. Or you could be a wise person. Listen, I said. None of this sounds like me. How about getting me a job in the plot factory? I think I'd be good at that. I'd get the hang of it really fast, I said.[1]

It makes you think, doesn't it—about an empty canvas upon which we can imagine infinite characters and plot lines for how our lives could play out? We might even test the waters—start over in a new country, switch careers after 20 years, change religions, leave everything we know and sail around the world—or just muse comfortably within the safety of our imagination. Each of those forays, real or imaginary, is an exploration between *something* and *something else*. What I want to explore here, however, is not something—but *nothing*.

If we look at our lives, and other people's lives, we see a lot of activity and behavior that clearly doesn't work and is counterproductive. Why do we do that? If even before we do it, we know it's not going to work, why do we do it? The answer is usually because we have some attachment to the significance of what we're experiencing or what we think it all means. It's like we tell ourselves, "Well, things are a particular way, therefore I've got to handle things a particular way." We don't realize that the level of the information that we're dealing with is microscopically limited against what's possible.

Another way of saying it: We get born, and we're taught whatever we're taught, the culture passes on to us whatever gets passed on, our families and educational systems teach us whatever we're supposed to learn. And we hold on tightly to all of it—because to be accepted, good, or at least well functioning, we need to know *something*. It seems, though, that we never really question the underpinnings of what we know.

We end up with a view of ourselves that we essentially just accept. We have a sense of how we developed this trait or that quirk, this conclusion or that belief. We say that life means this or that, or you mean this or that, or my life is about this, but it should be about that. Kurt Vonnegut says in his book, *Deadeye Dick*, "I have caught life. I have come down with life. I was a wisp of undifferentiated nothingness, and then a little peephole opened quite suddenly. Light and sound poured in. Voices began to describe me and my surroundings. Nothing they said could be appealed. They said I was a boy named Rudolph Waltz, and that was that. They said the year was 1932, and that was that. They said I was in Midland City, Ohio, and that was that. They never shut up. Year after year they piled detail upon detail. They do it still. You know what they say now? They say the year is 1982, and that I am fifty years old.... Blah, blah, blah."[2]

Like Vonnegut's character, we may see that *who we are* came from what we were told, places we lived, and experiences we had—mostly when we were young and learning to deal with life. Along the way we made decisions to get through the circumstances we encountered, let's say, when we were 5, or 7, or 10 years old. Those decisions worked for us at the time, so we kept them around, and incorporated them into our ways of being. A kind of absurdity lies underneath acting as if who we are today is just a compilation of those ways of being that we put together way back then. Obviously, we're not really stuck with those ways of being—also, it's not inherently who we are. So the question becomes, *who inherently are we?* Maybe nothing—maybe there's no inherent way that we are. Perhaps in the underpinnings, there's this...nothingness.

We live in a world where meaning is attached to almost everything, but not as if we were the ones who put the meaning out there. We think it's *really* out there. If we remove meaning from life, then what is really out there? Maybe nothing. This encounter with nothing can be a difficult task for any human being, because we are wired to perceive all phenomena as meaningful. There are things out there: the sun, a road, a tree, a lamp, a friend. But what does the tree mean? Does the tree mean, *oh, that tree was placed here so I can sit underneath it and read*? Or might the tree just be a tree? What if we just for one moment strip out the particular meaning we've added to a tree being there, or to things that have happened in our lives, and then ask, what's really out there? Perhaps there's nothing inherently out there–things are just the way things are.

This notion of nothing or nothingness has been pondered by philosophers over the centuries. "Nothing" puts us face-to-face with the malleability of our present meanings–it is antithetical to the common-sense view of our culture. It is our structure of meaning that defines our individual relationship with the world and gives us a confident hold on our identity–which we grew up holding as fundamental to healthy human living. To encounter *nothing* as a freedom, we must pass through and beyond our initial and natural resistance to the very idea.

One of the essential elements of Landmark's technology is that it makes this transformative encounter with *nothing* available. *Nothing* is elusive–nothing, as nothing, disappears. While we may get it and then lose it again and again, getting it even once is an experience we never get over. The importance of an encounter with *nothing* lies in the fundamental relationship of nothing to *being*. *Nothing*, or *non-being*, is the other side of being; and just as we cannot fully understand light until we have experienced dark, a full openness to what's available in being human demands an equivalent openness to nothing–an essential element of transformation. When we are able to access *nothing*, we are able to create, design, and live with a freedom that's not available when we create from *something*.

But the *nothing* that's available for us to experience in Landmark's programs is not nothing as a negation of self. A transformative experience of *nothing* does not do away with our identity–our identity is simply no longer seen as defining, in any way, the limits of what it is to be human–in the same way that our height or gender doesn't define it. The possibility of being human is open to being created. The message isn't that we *are* nothing–"being nothing" is an oxymoron, and an identity is as necessary for the game of life as a playing piece is for the game of Monopoly. The *nothing* we are speaking of here is nothing *as a clearing* for self, a clearing that frees the self from its own self-imposed restrictions, leaving us with the full range of possibility available to us in being human.

Landmark Essay 3

When Ideals Masquerade as Possibility

NANCY ZAPOLSKI, PH.D.

From the words of poets throughout the ages to English author Zadie Smith's novel, *On Beauty*, to novelist and philosopher Umberto Eco's comments, beauty gets a lot of ink. "Beauty is a mess, a sinkhole, a trap," says Eco. "Approach it philosophically, and you risk getting bogged down in questions of idealism, empiricism, subjectivity, and objectivity. Plato began the conversation, Kant tried to finish it. Take a cultural run at it, and you're stumbling over issues of relativism, where nothing is either beautiful or ugly but time, class, nation, or ethnicity makes it so."

These issues of relativism, of arbitrary ideals and standards, become so real and unquestioned, they become powerful yet mostly invisible determinants that shape our lives.

We traffic daily in concepts like beauty, success, generosity, intelligence—they hold a place in every peer group, every community, every culture around the world. They exist as ideals, expectations, and standards. While their specific expressions and definitions vary from place to place, situation to situation—in one country beautiful means Rubenesque, in another, extremely thin—we all strive for ideals. They are the measures we use every day—to see where we stand, how we fit in, how we stack up.

Ideals have enormous practical value. They can be powerful catalysts motivating us to open new frontiers, excel in sports, establish such principles as justice and democracy, or set benchmarks for educational, medical, and technological progress. They permeate every aspect of our lives. Ideals can awaken passion and an urgency that calls forth excellence, persistence, and going beyond our perceived limits, allowing for something new and surprising to emerge.

There is also a downside. One that is subtle, grows, and over time can take hold.

The dictionary defines "ideal" as being a model or archetype, something thought of as perfect, or exactly as one would wish. When we are driven by the ideal, we almost by definition fall short. Holding on to an ideal, while spurring us on, can also keep us from seeing what else is possible. We can't imagine what we might create or do because we are held captive by the particular ideal we have in our minds.

An ideal can become a "failed possibility"–a something or a commitment that wasn't achieved, but one that stayed around as something that is not possible, now or perhaps ever. A failed possibility is something like when we make up our minds to handle something in a particular way and we don't–for example, we mean to be compassionate, but we find ourselves judging; we want to speak up, go for the promotion, make our contribution, but find ourselves not taking action.

When that happens we see ourselves as having failed in some way. It's not just that a *thing* failed, but that *we* failed. To the degree that the characteristics or properties with which we identify ourselves are ideals–beautiful, magnanimous, successful, whatever–we decide we don't have what it takes, and who we are can become diminished.

Now, throw into the mix "expectations." Expectations might be thought of as a possibility that we've destroyed as a possibility, because we counted on it. If, for example, we really study and think we're going to get a high grade on an exam, or we train hard to make the cut for a sports team, but it doesn't pan out—what lived for us as a possibility, but failed, can leave us questioning ourselves, our character, and the stuff of which we are made. We then try to go out and create a new possibility, but it's against a backdrop that negates it. We stop trusting the possibilities we create; we turn down the dials, adjust, and accommodate—we settle for less. Possibilities devolve into ideals, and ideals begin to masquerade as possibility. Our power lessens.

How we relate to our setbacks and circumstances has everything to do with what's possible. Responses like "it's not my fault," "I didn't invent the rules," or "it just happened that way" might seem legitimate but leave us paying a price—the price is a loss of power. Responsibility—acknowledging our cause in the matter, seeing where we have been inauthentic, taking whatever actions we need to take, and telling the truth about it—begins to restore that power.

It's not that the ideal or expectation is bad, by any means, it's collapsing the two and relating to them in the same way that power is lost. As shown in the diagram,

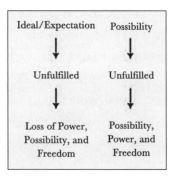

an *expectation* or *ideal unfulfilled* leads to a lack of power, where a *possibility unfulfilled* still leaves an opening for possibility–and there is no loss of power or freedom.

Access to restoring our power resides in language. When we're clear that we've got something to say about who we are, we can separate out our interpretation from the circumstance–the disparity between something that happened, and the possibility of who we are. What we say to ourselves and about ourselves, silently and out loud, once or a million times, shapes our possibilities for being. Our ideals, standards, and expectations occur in language. Our reluctance, accommodation, and powerlessness occur in language. But language is also the home–the only home–of possibility. What determines whether possibility (a creative act) or an ideal masquerading as possibility will carry the day is up to each of us. The choice is ours.

Landmark Essay 4

The Power of Context and the Courage to Create

JOE DIMAGGIO, M.D.

Football in The Netherlands, tennis in the U.K., cricket in India–whether we read about it in the news, watch it on television, or sit in the stands, we know the feeling:

The instant the ball rolled between Bill Buckner's legs New England broke into a collective moan. Mets fans uncontrollably squealed with glee. Then it was over and there was only silence. Local taverns packed with people watching Game 6 of the 1986 World Series suddenly filled with malice and fans walked away leaving money on the table. Boston's long awaited world championship was there–and then it was gone. All that remained for Red Sox fans was the grim certainty of an inevitable loss in Game 7 and more proof that this was not the year.

The Red Sox didn't have a chance. This team and its fans didn't recover from such defeats. Never had and never would.[1]

Sports fans everywhere have a tendency to get attached to the games, the players, the seasons. The players, larger than life, are personal heroes; they pull the curtain back on greatness and let their fans play a part. But in Boston, that was not to be. For many years, whatever momentary hope Red Sox fans may have had—thinking perhaps *this time* they could win—was eclipsed by their team's continual string of losses. It was the conversation in their neighborhoods, their schools, their families, even among their politicians. They knew they'd blown it in 1918 by trading Babe Ruth to the Yankees, and since then they just couldn't get back to the top. The state of affairs for Red Sox fans was a hard, cold reality—*the way it was.* The context hovering over them was that "the Sox" weren't winners. (Luckily, I was a Yankees fan.)

We're defining *context* here to mean "a fundamental set of assumptions"—assumptions that are not recognized as assumptions, and that go unquestioned—in which the *world happens.* When people thought the earth was flat (an analogy that grows old but never dies), that was a context or worldview that limited perception and behavior—how those folks saw the horizon, how far toward the edge they sailed, and so on. Similarly, our way of being a man or a woman, and the possibilities available to us, are given by the assumptions embedded in our culture, our language, and times in which we live. A girl born in the U.S. today would likely inherit a very different possibility for being a woman than a girl born in the 1930s or '40s–would she be a dot-com mogul or running for president?

So if you consider the premise that the whole world happens *inside* of the assumptions we hold true (and if you do the math), what becomes apparent is that *contexts are a mighty and decisive force*. Contexts come to us by default, and we live our lives essentially unaware of their existence and of their far-reaching influence. It's like wearing blinders–we don't see the *contexts* themselves, we see only what they allow. These *default contexts* determine our worldview: what's possible and not, what's true and false, what's right and wrong, what we think we can and can't do. They travel with us–wherever *we* are, *they* are–shaping our behavior, our choices, our lives.

Just as these *default contexts* can be what keeps us limited and stuck, *created* or *invented contexts* can allow for freedom and power. We're not talking, however, about substituting one context over another, or finding a *better* context or the *right* context. Rather, it's about becoming aware of and responsible for *whatever* context we are functioning inside of, and realizing that we have the power not only to invent contexts, but to move freely among them.

History is strewn with examples of times when major advances happened as a result of new contexts being created. Democracy, equality, relativity, human rights–new ways of understanding the world–were at some point, *newly distinguished contexts*. The Copernican revolution abruptly dislodged humans from the center of the universe, ushering in modern astronomy and the scientific revolution. Newton *invented* gravity (certainly, before Newton, there was a physical force, but he transformed the possibility of that force), enabling us to understand and interact more powerfully with the physical universe. Einstein *created* relativity–a context that catalyzed modern physics and tells us how nature behaves on the scale of apples, planets, galaxies, and on up. At one time, human rights, as we think of them today, simply didn't exist. Kings had rights, priests had rights, and the ruling class had rights, but the majority of human beings–and often, certain specific groups within a society–did not. In each of these examples, some person or a group of people saw through or past "the way things were," or the way they "seemed to have to be." The act of doing so, and saying so, reshaped the course of events and redefined human experience from then on. And we then began living into those possibilities and the "truth" of the world was transformed.

And so it is with being human. We take for granted that things *are* a particular way; we think it is our circumstances, our cultures, the content of our lives that determine our experience. And if we want some kind of change in our lives, we usually go to work on changing the circumstances–essentially moving the *content* around. (Not surprisingly, we then end up living *content-driven lives.*)

Living from an *invented context* has just as much impact and command value as living from a *default context*–the difference, however, is the difference between a life of *predictability* and a life of *possibility.* The answer to the question "what's possible in being human?" doesn't need to be looked at through a *default* lens. Seeing past our old assumptions about "the way things have been" or the way we thought "they had to be" and creating a *context* of our own choosing alters the very nature of what's possible–and the truth of "our" world gets transformed.

An *invented context* is essentially a *realm of possibility.* And we have the wherewithal to create that realm simply by our *saying so.* Language–what we say (silently or aloud, once or repeatedly, to ourselves or to others)–has the power to shape reality. When we know our conversations constitute *who we are*, it shifts our relationship to the world. The shift does not necessarily get rid of the lens or filters or mindsets per se, but what occurs is that those old assumptions simply stop defining who we are. *Context* known in that way is never inherited, never a matter of acculturation, never a matter of something we picked up, never a matter of accident–it's always and only a matter of our choosing. Choice is a uniquely human condition. "The stone and the tiger have no choice of life: the stone must gravitate and the tiger must pounce. Only human beings are faced with the mind-boggling responsibility of having, at each and every moment of their lives, to choose what to do and what to be. It is both a necessity and an invitation."[2]

In 2007 the Red Sox became World Series Champions for the second time in three years–and had the most dominant postseason run in history.

Landmark
Essay 5

The Unravelling of In-Order-Tos

NANCY ZAPOLSKI, PH.D.

Many of us experience, from the moment we awake, a background hum of *concern*–for one thing, for many things, sometimes for everything. It's as if almost all of life comes wrapped in some sort of concern. The hum has been with us for as long as we can remember and can come to us in various frequencies–a feverish pitch to the faintest of whispers. We might be concerned about being heard or liked, finding the right mate, getting ahead. Here's a tale of a child's concern–but one that is by no means exclusive to childhood:

"I had always wanted to be in a club. The first one was founded by my older sister for the sole purpose of letting her friends in and keeping my friends and me out. The clubhouse was our parents' bridge table, with a bed sheet thrown over it, but no matter. The more exclusive and restricted the membership, the greater our desire to get in. And the more we sought ingress, the greater the power the club held over us. That's what made a club a club.

"It wasn't until I kicked and screamed, and my parents intervened, that the sheet finally was lifted and we were admitted to the inner sanctum. Naturally, the moment we were, the club's exclusivity seemed to evaporate. In fact, it was no longer even a club—just the space under the sheet covering the card table.

"Not much has changed since then. As adults (more or less), we're enthralled by closed doors and velvet ropes, held at bay by guest-list checkers, gatekeepers, and membership committees. What's the matter with us? Are we social masochists? Is our need to belong so great that it trumps self-respect? Yes, of course! And not just belong, but belong to something just far enough above our regular stations so as to elevate our opinion of ourselves, if not others'."[1]

When do these ever-present, never silent concerns begin? With the very early awareness that something can and most likely will go wrong. This awareness arrives early in life, long before we were able to sort out whether having concerns was even valid. When we first thought something might go wrong—whether whatever happened was truly threatening or just apparently so—the *world of concerns* was born.

This world of concerns finds a welcoming host in us. It takes residence, sets up house, slowly begins to add mass to itself—and becomes something to which we unwittingly pay heed. We even develop a concern for the success of our concerns. Over time, our concerns occur as if they're just part of who we are—an idiosyncratic part of ourselves, a personality quirk, but for sure something we act as if we're stuck with, like a genetic or hard-wired trait.

Growing up, like any child, I had my share of concerns. Not about getting into a club under the card table, but about being "better" and doing things more perfectly than my sister. That's what mattered to me at that particular time in my childhood. In the eyes of whoever was looking, I wanted to be seen as the best—at getting good grades, at baking cookies, at whatever I did. I studied books and my peers to learn what I could *in order to* be perfect, better-than, recognized, and loved. But how perfect I was or wasn't didn't occur for me as a concern I was responding to—it was just me being *who I was.*

Being perfect wasn't easy. The landscape kept shifting. As life went on, it was harder and harder for me to be perfect. I realized that I wasn't the most loved sibling, or the only smart girl at school. Eventually the need to be better-than and perfect, day after day, was no longer as enchanting or compelling as it once was. I just wanted to relax and give up the push. Truthfully, I longed to enjoy my sister, watch her excel, be her buddy–but my need to come out ahead took precedence.

Stopping at times like that to question our behavior, yet continuing the behavior, rationalizing and justifying as we go along, seems pretty surprising. Why would we enact behaviors in order to get something we realize we don't really want or need?

Most *in-order-tos* are a strategy for dealing with some concern. And often, whatever initiated the concern was so long ago that we have no real memory of it. How we responded to what happened back then worked back then, so we carry it forward with no awareness of why *or* that it's even an "it"–it's just *how/who we are.* As Charles Dickens put it, "The forces that affect our lives, the influences that mold and shape us, are often like whispers in a distant room, teasingly indistinct, apprehended only with difficulty." Yet these whispers, which we can barely apprehend, still have the power to shape our lives today.

When much of what we do is a response *in order to* deal with some concern, that's not great news because it's as if we don't know or do anything just for itself— and that keeps us from being present. The ultimate kind of bad news, however, is to find out that we will never get enough of whatever it is—honest enough, genuine enough, contributing enough, savvy enough, wise enough—to quell our concerns. If that's the case, the natural state of being whole and complete cannot happen. In order to deal with, adapt to, and accommodate to that, we put together various *ways of being*—and there you have it, that's our life experience. This dynamic occurs over and over, and we keep being driven by it—it comes with the territory of being human.

While we may not have been aware of this dynamic before, now we are. Being aware of what we weren't aware of, and being responsible for it, leaves us free to choose and free to create possibility. The power to choose and the power to create possibility reside in language. Language is far more than just a tool that describes or represents reality. To know the power of language, other than mere words, essentially requires a transformation from knowing ourselves as who we have considered ourselves to be, our identities, to knowing ourselves as our word—as "what we say." With that transformation comes knowing ourselves in a new way, that of honoring our speaking—honoring our word as ourselves. It is in the relationship each of us has to our "word" where the rubber meets the road. If we are willing to honor our word as ourselves, we give our word the power to alter the way life occurs for us.

Being one's word only exists as a possibility. When we have created a possibility, it's not something we're trying to do. Nor is it a matter of in-order-to. Questions like "will it happen or not," or "do we need to do 'X' in-order-to get to 'Y'," aren't really relevant to possibility. When we create a new possibility for ourselves, it does exist. It's present in the world–not as a physical phenomenon, but as possibility.

Landmark Essay 6

With Transformation Comes Big Shoes

Joe DiMaggio, M.D.

"We are not like the social insects," writes Lewis Thomas, biologist and physician, "which have only one way of doing things... We are coded differently, not just for ... *go or no go*, but also for *maybe*, plus *what the heck, let's give it a try*. We are in for one surprise after another if we just keep at it... There is no end to what we might do."

And there is indeed no end to what we might do. We have the power to transform the quality of our lives–no matter when and no matter what the circumstances. *If that's so, well then, what the heck, why not?*

45

The *why not* is mostly because people don't know what's really possible—and because we don't know that, we oftentimes play for low stakes. If we took our day and divided it up between the stuff that really made a difference, and the rest of the stuff (not between what was important and what was unimportant, but the stuff that *really made a difference* and all the rest), what would we see?

Remember, for example, when you were a teenager, the stuff that was REALLY IMPORTANT. Remember when your parents said you couldn't go to a dance, or you had to be home at a certain time and couldn't stay out an extra hour. Remember how really, really important that was? Now, as adults, most of us forget that "important" things are pretty much just like that— they seem important at the time, but a week, a month, or a year later, what was the big deal?

This brings up for me something about my teenage step-daughter, Alex, that she, my wife, and I wanted to share in this article. Alex has taken The Landmark Forum for Young People and for Teens. She knows what it takes to play powerfully in the game of life and she has created very big shoes for herself—mostly.

Once in a while she likes to pretend the shoes aren't hers. I remember an argument she had with my wife, Diane, over a curfew agreement. Afterward, Diane and I both thought the issues had been sorted out, that they had been discussed fully, and agreed to. Alex went off to school the next morning, but she did not come home when we expected her. It got later and later. We were upset and enormously concerned for her safety and well-being. Once she did get home, we sat down together to discuss it. For her, the issue was more than merely conversation about curfew. It was about things that were HUGELY IMPORTANT in her world—her peers, how she looked to them, her sense of independence, and being in control of her own life.

Everything got sorted through—and what was left was that she knew that all of it could have been sorted out without a struggle, or any "looking bad" with her peers, or any upset with us—but to do so, she would have had to live up to the person she knew herself to be. She, however, chose not to go down that path. She preferred to be part of the same conversation her peers were having, to not communicate, to be defiant even when she knew that it wasn't necessary and wouldn't get her what she really wanted. When it was all over, we talked about the courage it takes to live in a transformed way, to know what it requires, to know that under any circumstance we each have a choice, to act and live from that reality.

That's the story of a teenager. But I also know from interacting with many adults that this issue of living in a way that's consistent with who we now know ourselves to be, of filling the shoes that we can't pretend aren't big, doesn't stop when our teenage years are behind us. It goes right into adulthood.

Under many circumstances, we aren't willing to stand up for living a transformed life. In some circumstances, we tell ourselves that's not important to us, that it's enough just to get by. We get so wrapped up in our own concerns, particular positions, or points of view that the idea of getting ourselves to a place where things can be resolved in the moment seems untenable. If somebody had a magic powder to come and sprinkle on us, in those moments, and just through that, we could be transformed, we might say, "No, thanks–I don't want any!"

We might hear ourselves saying, "Don't let anything different, or even great, happen to me. Let me stay just like I am." And then we might spend a lot of time building up a justification for where we are–afraid to give up the leaky life boat that's so familiar, to take a chance on getting into one with no leaks. And our justifications will be rational and intelligent–just like my step-daughter's initial response, and like all the thousands of reasons people use every day to justify staying where they are.

Living a transformed life takes courage. People often think of courage only as what is called for in a moment of crisis, but that's not the case. Courage is called for on a day-to-day, moment-to-moment basis, even when there's nothing urgent at stake. It is up to us to create our lives consistent with who we know ourselves to be—making what's at stake that which we say is at stake. It's the stand we take on ourselves. That stand then becomes who we are. Saying that something is at stake is a purely existential act. This business about freedom, this business about power, is really a product of a place to stand—not something that is out in front of us, that we're working on or measuring ourselves against. When we live consistent with what we say, we are being true to ourselves.

Transformation has the power to upset the status quo, to unseat us from "business as usual"—it gives us a platform for being all we can. To choose living a transformed life requires us to wrestle with our resistances, small and large, to come face to face with the angst of giving up our self-imposed limits, our mediocrity—but most important, to live consistent with what we know is possible. Transformation carries with it a wisdom and a knowing that we have a choice about who we are and the full range that is available to us in being human. With transformation comes big shoes.

Landmark Essay 7

Fear, Survival, and the Courage to Be

NANCY ZAPOLSKI, PH.D.

There was a forest at the beginning of fiction too. This one spread forever. Its canopy of branches covered the land. Up in its living roof birds flitted through greenness and bright air, but down between the trunks of the many trees there were shadows, there was dark. When you walked this forest your feet made rustling sounds, but the noises you made were not the only noises, oh no. Twigs snapped; breezes brought snatches of what might be voices. Lumpings and crashes in the undergrowth marked the passages of heavy things far off, or suddenly nearby. This was a populated wood. All wild creatures lived here, dangerous or benign according to their natures. And all the other travelers you had heard of were in the wood too: kings and knights, youngest sons and third daughters, simpletons and outlaws; a small girl whose bright hood flickered between the pine trees like a scarlet beacon, and a wolf moving on a different vector to intercept her at the cottage. Each traveled separately, because it was the nature of the forest that you were alone in it. It was the place in which by definition you had no companions, and no resources except your own uncertain self. It was the Wild, where relationship ceases, where connection is suspended. There would be encounters, of course....[1]

When we're young, things can get out of control pretty quickly. We experience danger as a distinct possibility that's "out there somewhere," and it becomes a notion that stays with us, at some level or another, throughout time. So from a very early age, we're kind of *on alert*. The idea that life can be dangerous doesn't go away just because we become (more rational) adults. And when we carry around the idea that life could be dangerous for many years, even the notion of *possibility* can seem, well... threatening.

When I was in high school, I loved to go with my girlfriends to weekly dances at our school. I was a pretty good dancer but uncoordinated in sports–that left me a bit self-conscious, and when I was asked to dance, I'd hesitate. I said things to myself like: "They might find out I'm not so great in sports," "They might make fun of me"–that whole barrage of self-censoring internal dialogue. When we give our fears rein, even the smallest moments can be daunting. Fears arise when we look back, and they arise when we look ahead. Fears arise about ourselves, and about our reception from others. Whatever their origins, they prevent us from living fully. Whether a threat is *real* (a situation where our survival is at stake–our security, our health, keeping our families safe) or *imagined* (a situation that *might* await us, something that *might* happen–or where we *might* be made to look foolish, for example), it is all about survival. Those moments of fear and anxiety– with the constriction in our chest, the fluttering of our hearts, the feelings of imminent danger or potential embarrassment–can be overwhelming, because we think some aspect of our survival is at stake.

Perhaps even more than sadness, anger, or disappointment, we find it difficult to deal with fear. Fear can keep us from participating, from doing what we're capable of–from experiencing and expressing the full range of possibility that's available to us in being human. The disempowerment, constraints, and stops, however, are not a function of the *experience of fear* but rather a function of the *meaning* we've added, and the decisions we made, at a particular time in the past. Another way of saying it is that it's not the fear that is operative, but the automatic way we collapse *something that happened* with *what we say it signifies*. It's that automaticity that keeps us stuck in place, and what has us lose our power. Old circumstances now have the power, not us.

When we stop going for it–when we step back, play it safe, or say we can't do something–we might avoid the experience of fear for the moment, but at the same time we are reinforcing where we're stuck. We're limiting our freedom, and cutting off possibility. Being alive includes risks, threats, and danger–the possibility of "bad" things happening is always there. But in planning our life to avoid those things, we're essentially avoiding life–obviously not the wisest way to be alive. The *Harvard Business Review* might not be where you'd expect to read about fear's pervasive presence, but the following appeared in a recent issue and I thought it apropos: "I get the willies when I see closed doors." That is the first line of Joseph Heller's *Something Happened*, one of the handful of superb novels about business. Heller's hero and narrator, Bob Slocum, a middling executive at an unnamed company, is driven nearly mad thinking that decisions might be made behind his back that could ruin his career and his life, or might merely change things that are, while odious to him, at least bearable. Without transparency, Slocum is a quivering wreck. He's not alone. As the second chapter begins, Slocum says, "In the office in which I work there are five people of whom I am afraid. Each of these five people is afraid of four people (excluding overlaps), for a total of twenty, and each of these twenty people is afraid of six people, making a total of one hundred and twenty people who are feared by at least one person." The company, in other words, is a pyramid of potential panic, ready to topple when someone whispers, "Jig's up."[2]

I'm always amazed how Heller gets right to the absurdity of a situation, this time pointing to the momentum that fear can generate all on its own. And it doesn't just automatically disappear because we'd like it to. But when we can separate out *what happened* from *the meanings we assigned,* we no longer have to be "at the effect" of whatever happened. We don't have to work on top of it, push it down, accommodate, or adapt to it. We survived the first time, the second, third, and so on—completing a past fear includes recognizing that we would *survive* if the past repeated itself. When we stop trying to resist the past happening again, things shift. In separating out *what happened* and the decisions we made back then, we clear up a lot of the disempowerment and lack of freedom.

There's a big difference between being realistic about what happened once, and being resigned or stuck that things *have to continue to be some way* now or that they just *are some way* or *they'll be that way again.* Instead of wishing we could change our past experience—a futile exercise—we have the freedom to choose our relationship to whatever it was, and that's the beginning of building power. That's the beginning of creating possibility. *Possibility* invites us into areas of creativity, of uncertainty, of paradox and surprise. It invites us to bring things into existence that haven't existed, take a step to one side or another, unsettle old realities. Our own identity, say, or the certainty of some fact, the behavior of others, or even the meaning of words can come to be seen and understood in new ways.

It takes enormous courage to try out new *ways of being* in the space where fear used to be, and by choosing to do so, we come to be authors of our own experience. Choosing requires courage—and courage leads to the ontological question of *being.* Courage is rooted in the whole breadth of human existence, and ultimately in the structure of *being* itself. Courage can show us what *being* is, and *being* can show us what courage is.

Landmark
Essay 8

Distinctions:
Access to the Prime
Terrain of Being

Joe DiMaggio, M.D.

Norman Cousins says, "The purpose of education and learning is to create a higher sense of the possible than would occur naturally." He goes on to say, "This must mean more than relieving the tension caused by confrontation with the unknown—it must mean developing a zestful capacity for dealing in abstractions and regarding abstractions as the prime terrain for exploration and discovery.... No abstraction, of course, is as potentially fruitful as the individual's knowledge of and access to himself."

Exploring abstractions and distinctions is indeed

prime terrain–the prime terrain of *being*, and the terrain on which Landmark's technology is based. The act of distinguishing–or as Cousins refers to it, "dealing in abstractions"–can give us the access, the malleability, the freedom to live a life of which we are the architect. Distinctions as we're referring to them here are *ontological* in nature–they address the *being* part of human beings rather than the *knowledge* part. Most Landmark programs consider the notion that our actions and interactions arise from our *way of being*, rather than from what we know. Our *ways of being*, unlike knowledge, aren't readily accessible to us. Knowledge is easily accessible just by going after it, we can increase it, refine it, etc. But it's the nature of "being" that we do not *know* it, we simply *are* it.

This "distinction" thing is worth grappling with, as it can give us access to *that which we are*. The grappling, however, can turn out to be slippery, because distinctions can never actually be pinned down. They have broad application, and perhaps most importantly allow us to address the "who we are" in the matter of what we know. They are at the nexus of Landmark's technology.

Renowned physicist Richard Feynman describes a set of experiments in which rats ran through mazes. In one, a long corridor had doors along both sides. Rats came in on one side and the researcher wanted to see if he could train the rats to go into the third door from wherever they entered, rather than going to the door where they found food the time before. To identify what factors made a difference in the rats' behavior, the researcher painted the doors, used chemicals to change the residual smells, blocked out the lighting and still the rats went where the food used to be. Finally, he covered the floor in sand and was able to fool the rats. From a scientific standpoint, Feynman thought this to be an A-number-one experiment, because it uncovered the clue that the rats were really using–not what a person might think they were using. This excellent experiment, though, was never referred to by others, because it didn't reveal anything about rats per se. It did, however, reveal the things you have to do to discover something *about* rats.[1]

That's where distinctions come into the picture–they give us an access to discover something *about* the nature of things, including our own nature. A distinction is more than a concept and different from a theory. Concepts might be included in a distinction, but concepts aren't a crucial element of distinctions. The power of a distinction isn't located in any particular place, or even in what is known. Distinctions can't be memorized, appropriated, or willed into being. They are not additive, nor do they include learning a series of parts that are then assembled into a whole. Distinctions exist in language, but not in any particular word or set of words, so they can never quite be captured within a concept or description. Also, distinctions differ from definitions. Definitions provide limits; distinctions generate possibilities. Distinctions become powerfully present only through a series of hints or pointing-tos, yet once present, open whole new worlds.

Imagine, for example, what the world would be like without the distinction "number." Would mathematics, engineering, science exist? Would we have bridges or buildings, air travel, be able to bake a cake, reach the moon? What the distinction "number" makes available is so ubiquitous that it's hard to imagine life without it. You could say the same for "gravity," or even "human rights," a distinction that continues to evolve as time goes on.

Distinguishing implies a bringing forth from the undifferentiated background, a calling forward, so to speak. Kids learn to ride bikes when they are able to "distinguish" balance. Until then, no amount of explanation, instruction, encouragement, however helpful, can actually do the trick. Learning to ride a bicycle occurs when we bring forth from the background that group of sensations which is distinguished as "balance." No kid riding a bicycle is trying to plan, figure out, or remember the distinction "balance." They are simply riding–visiting buddies in other neighborhoods, doing wheelies, or just living in an expanded world where balance and a new mobility are now theirs. When the distinction *balance* is present an entire world that was not previously there becomes available.

Like the experiment Feynman referred to, distinctions don't tell us why we do what we do as human beings, but give us a certain access–a portal to ourselves. In the process of distinguishing "identity," for example, we see that *who we consider ourselves to be* is essentially put together by default–that a series of decisions and reactions, seemingly appropriate at the time, have come to define our *identity–who we are,* how we act, our very nature. Once "identity" is distinguished and actually seen for what it is, at that moment we see that *who we are* and *who we've thought ourselves to be* are not set, fixed, or any particular way, but rather are malleable and open to being invented. Old, unexamined decisions, notions, and *ways of being* stop defining who we are.

Distinguishing *identity,* and the extraordinary world that makes possible, is just one example of the power of distinctions. Developing a competency in creating distinctions gives us enormous access to power and effectiveness in any area of life. Just as "balance" allows for riding a bicycle, and "number" allows for engineering, distinctions in the realm of *being* allow for living a life of which we are the architect. Distinctions transform reality–they are the prime terrain of *being.*

Landmark Essay 9

Inventing New Futures—Altering Old, Limiting Realities

NANCY ZAPOLSKI, PH.D.

Two stories: The first takes place in the Los Angeles Police Department, the other within the rarified art world of New York.

A rookie cop on the Los Angeles police force reported for duty on a vice squad, and found out that his new precinct held an unusual lottery. It turned out that this precinct included a really terrible beat, in a dangerous section of the city. None of the vice cops ever wanted to patrol this area—so after years of fielding objections, the precinct captain had finally come up with a solution he thought was fair.

Every night, as the shift started, the captain held up a bag of marbles. Every marble in the bag was black, except for one. Filing slowly to the front of the room, each cop pulled a marble from the bag and from the marble learned his fate. Whichever cop drew the single odd-colored marble had to brace himself for a descent into the neighborhood they dreaded. The atmosphere was stressed and miserable—moments of happy camaraderie were rare. The rookie soon found himself dragging his feet about going to work. Twice he pulled the odd-colored marble and discovered the beat to be every bit as unsavory as everyone had said. But he managed to survive it.

One night the rookie walked to the front of the marble line, dumped out the marbles, and deliberately chose the odd-colored marble. The next night he did it again. Night after night, he specifically requested that one marble. He no longer worried about losing the marble lottery. Now, for better or worse, his fate was in his own hands.[1] What he had experienced as enormously stressful, he chose to transform. Through his actions and example, the mood and morale in the precinct began to shift.

Across the continent, in New York City, a curator of the Museum of Modern Art spoke of the impact the advent of modern art had on the traditional art world. He said that "modern art, from Picasso's scrambled faces to Andy Warhol's soup cans–acts of imagination with no supporting consensus and only the tiniest circle of initial understanding–produced [enormous] changes [in the way we look not only at art, but] at the world. It ignored traditional texts, sidestepped familiar standards, and required people to make judgments without the comfort of stable rules and categories, and to navigate in seas of uncertainty, even absurdity, without a map."[2] Critics have said of Picasso's "Les Demoiselles d'Avignon" that it is "a deliberate throw of the gauntlet to the entire history of art. You can see it again and again and still be struck dumb by its audacity, its freshness and its courage."[3] And, "It changed art more than any other. Before it, paintings at least had to pretend to be decorative and cogent. Afterward anything went."[4]

Both the realities that existed in the L.A. precinct and the art circles of New York had amassed years of agreement. One fostered a reality of anxiety, stress, and low morale. The other set the standard for purchase price, reputation, and the au courant. In each situation, long-standing realities of *the way it was* were altered by a new conversation.

What was "real" in each of these cases?

Most of us think of language as describing *a reality that's out there*–other people, things, the universe, even ourselves. We talk about ourselves and we say things like, "I am this way or that, I am outgoing/I am cautious." We talk about ourselves and others almost as if we were objects to be described. That's not an inappropriate or incorrect use of language. It is, though, just one use of language. Language describes, but language also has the power to create. It can bring new worlds into being—worlds that may start off not as real. Possibility is not real at its origin—it's something we create as real, and then stand for as a reality.

Richard Rorty, contemporary philosopher, makes this point: "We need to make a distinction between the claim that the world is out there and the claim that truth is out there. To say that the world is out there— that it is not our creation—is to say that most things are the effects of causes and do not include [us]. Truth, however, cannot be *out there*—cannot exist independently of [us]."

"The world is out there, but descriptions of the world are not. Only descriptions of the world can be true or false. The world on its own—unaided by [language] of human beings—cannot. [If] we could ever become reconciled to the idea that most of reality is indifferent to our descriptions of it and that [we are] created by [language], then we should at last [know] that truth is made rather than found. The world does not speak. Only we do."

In Landmark we say that the reality, conditions, and

circumstances of the future do not yet exist as facts; they only exist as a product of the conversations we're in, we're having, and in fact *are*. Both in the case of the rookie cop and the modern artists, the introduction of and standing for a new conversation shifted the existing reality–life's possibilities and actualities were altered.

People who act out of inspired action do so by creating a possibility–articulating a future in such a way that it alters the way the present occurs. And because the present is now different, people act differently. Because people act in a way that is consistent with a new future, that future can then become possible.... But of course, as with any uncharted territory, there are inevitably gaps, stops and starts, missing bits. At these times, when there are gaps or something is or seems missing, it's missing not like an invalidation, but like a possibility.

An example of *something missing,* but *like a possibility* comes up in Picasso's juxtaposition of classic western art with African art as he created "Les Demoiselles." He wasn't all that confident about what he had done. The more he identified the abstracting quality of tribal art, the more he floundered and kept modifying the painting, sensing something was missing. Adding tribal masks, for him, was "a calculated risk, taken very late in the game."[5] For many years–until the painting was recognized as a modernist triumph—Picasso insisted *something was missing.* "'Les Demoiselles' holds within it a touching doubt, the angst of modern art as well as its trail to the future."[5]

Living in the face of a possibility often can carry with it that doubt or angst and can sometimes be difficult—difficult in the ways poetry, music, or a deep intimacy can be difficult, because it doesn't explain, it doesn't rationalize, it doesn't describe, and it doesn't define. Even at its earliest stages, possibility leaves us with power and freedom, and once fulfilled, is no longer a possibility—it is a reality that allows for whole new futures.

Landmark
Essay 10

Stepping Outside the Swirl—The Courage to be Authentic

JOE DIMAGGIO, M.D.

"One afternoon, in the middle of a particularly boring grammar class, my English teacher set aside her book and took nominations for the best song on our local Top 40 radio station. For the first time that year, all hands were in the air. There was no 'right answer' to a question of personal taste, or so I thought until she eventually called on me, and I announced my choice and that it was not only the best song in the Top 40 but possibly the best song ever.... What I remember is not my recommendation so much as the silence that followed it, an absence of agreement I can only describe as deafening.

"The first time I heard the song, I was hooked.... I

bought it and played it over and over again. The song satisfied me on every level, but if nobody else liked it, I guessed that I didn't, either. That evening, alone in my room, I found that I was too ashamed to listen to my record, or even to look at it, really. It reminded me of my wretched eagerness to please. From this point on, whenever someone asked my opinion, I would turn the question around, and then proceed accordingly. If the person I was with loved game shows and Deep Purple, then so would I, and if I was caught contradicting myself—watching or listening to something I'd sworn to have hated—I would claim to be doing research, or to be enjoying the thing for its very badness. You could do this, I learned, and people would forgive you, consider you interesting, even. *Having spent my life trying to fit the will of others, I was unable to distinguish between what I enjoyed and what I thought I should enjoy.*"[1]

We are all familiar with the old imperative "To thine own self be true," and clear that much would be resolved if only we operated consistently with it, but the pull for getting approval from others and the need to fit in is a strong one. Even when we're fully aware that we're being inauthentic, and know that we don't really believe in what we're doing or saying, we still *act* as if we do—because we're afraid we might risk losing approval of some kind. Even though we know the standards we've set for ourselves are impossible to realize, we still keep trying—we hide our perceived shortcomings, or pretend they don't exist. In doing so, we unwittingly add yet another layer of inauthenticity.

It's hard to be at ease when we have to keep up a pretense and not be true to ourselves in some way. Yet it's not as if we woke up one morning and intentionally said, "Gee, I think I'm going to act inauthentically today. What my life's going to be about is *looking good* and *avoiding looking bad*." This way of being is just kind of automatically there. Every time we opt for *looking good* or *avoiding looking bad* over what's actually true for us, inauthenticity creeps in and we compromise who we are.

We don't much like thinking of ourselves as being inauthentic, but we live in societies today in which the name of the game is to "make it," to "fit in," to "look good," so a great deal of what we think and do becomes shaped by a kind of cultural commitment to that. That pull or gravitational force is an ontological phenomenon, not a psychological one—it's the *already/ always condition* of being human (a term which kind of speaks for itself). This condition is ubiquitous—it influences everything: How we see and respond to situations, what we're concerned with, what's important to us. While we might think we are responding in true, authentic ways, what is actually happening is that our responses are essentially just a fallout of that *already/*

always condition. And it is against that pull—the enormous gravitational force of that condition—that we attempt to be authentic.

When we compromise, even in the tiniest of matters, it's easier for those compromises to become more and more commonplace; we begin to feel as if doing that is a normal and O.K. way of behaving. Over time, bit by bit, this erodes our sense of self. It's like stirring one drop of red paint into a can of white. The paint may turn only the palest shade of pink, and while that might seem barely noticeable—no matter what we say about it—the paint is no longer what it was. Similarly, when the wholeness and completeness of *who we are* is jeopardized in some way, albeit imperceptible at first, our sense of ourselves gets obscured, making it harder to return to *who we are.* When that begins, there's really no starting point to become ourselves—it's all flailing around.

To be authentic requires putting aspects of our present *ways-of-being* on the line—letting go of pretenses, letting things show themselves in new ways, and acknowledging whatever inauthenticity is at play. The *possibility* of fully being ourselves occurs in proportion to our being authentic; said another way, it occurs in proportion to the degree we own our inauthentic ways of being. In not owning them, we essentially resign ourselves to inauthenticity staying around. Living with a pretense, or being afraid that some aspect of ourselves might be found out, precludes any real freedom. We live, rather, with a kind of fabricated freedom—a large price to pay.

Sartre said that facing one's freedom can be terrifying and uncomfortable—because facing it makes one feel insecure, and inevitably produces some level of anguish. Hence, we are constantly tempted to live inauthentically, pretending to ourselves that we are not free. To maintain this pretense, we try to convince ourselves that our actions are determined—by our character, our circumstances, our nature, or whatever. The last thing we want to admit is that our actions are determined only by our free, unconstrained choices.[2]

Being authentic—stepping outside of the swirl of the *already/always condition*—requires courage. Humorist Josh Billings said, "This undertaking is not only the most difficult thing to do, but the most inconvenient as well." In being authentic, the *already/always condition* becomes stripped of its power and is no longer the determining force in shaping who we are. Here, the context for the question "who am I?" shifts from flailing about, trying to find ourselves somewhere *out there*, to a *context of creation*. This is more difficult, because there is no zeitgeist to read, no template to follow, no known path to success. It's a blank slate. It's a matter of courage—a matter of *creating* possibility. It gets made up as we go along, and it is this shift that makes available to us the full possibility of being human.

> *If I am not, I miss the point of my life, I miss what being human is for me.*
>
> — CHARLES TAYLOR

Endnotes

ESSAY 1

1. Philip Roth, *The Counterlife*. New York: Farrar, Straus, Giroux, 1986.

ESSAY 2

1. Margaret Atwood, *The Tent*. New York: Nan A. Talese/ Doubleday, 2006.

2. Kurt Vonnegut, *Deadeye Dick*. New York: Dell, 1982.

ESSAY 4

1. Glenn Stout, *Boston Baseball*, September 2004.

2. Harry Eyres, "Tyranny of Choice," *Financial Times*, November 2, 2007 (citing José Ortega y Gasset, in his essay "The Mission of the Librarian").

ESSAY 5

1. Tom Connor, "No Admittance," *Town & Country*, February 2006.

Essay 7

1. Francis Spufford, *The Child That Books Built: A Life in Reading*. New York: Picador, 2002.

2. Thomas A. Stewart, "Seeing Things," *Harvard Business Review*, February, 2008.

Essay 8

1. Richard P. Feynman, Ralph Leighton (contributor), and Edward Hutchings (editor), *"Surely You're Joking, Mr. Feynman!" (Adventures of a Curious Character)*. New York: W.W. Norton, 1985.

Essay 9

1. "Rookie cop" story adapted from Tom Robbins, *Wild Ducks Flying Backward: The Short Writings of Tom Robbins*. New York: Bantam Books, 2005.

2. Kirk Varnedoe, "Entering the Software Century," *ARTnews*, September 1992.

3. Thomas Hoving, "Nothing Like This Picasso," *Los Angeles Times*, May 8, 2007.

4. Michael Kimmelman, "Picasso's 'Demoiselles d'Avignon,' " *New York Times*, May 6, 2007.

5. Jackie Wullschlager, "The day modern art was invented: Picasso's Demoiselles," *Financial Times*, January 5, 2007.

Essay 10

1. David Sedaris (editor), "Introduction," *Children Playing Before a Statue of Hercules*. New York: Simon & Schuster, 2005.

2. Adapted from Raymond Martin and John Barresi, *The Rise and Fall of Soul and Self: An Intellectual History of Personal Identity*. New York: Columbia University Press, 2008.

About Landmark
Education

Landmark Education is a global leader in the field of training and development, offering courses and seminars that are innovative, effective, and immediately relevant. The Landmark Forum, the foundation of all Landmark Education's programs, is designed to bring about a fundamental shift or transformation in what is possible in people's lives.

Participants in The Landmark Forum and Landmark Education's other courses, seminars, and programs see new possibilities for effective action in everyday matters. People are able to achieve higher standards of excellence and to think and act beyond existing views and limits–in their personal lives, relationships, and wider communities of interest.

Landmark Education's courses, seminars, and programs are offered in more than 122 cities around the world. Graduates of The Landmark Forum often participate in additional programs that present a wide range of topics relevant to living everyday life powerfully, including: relationships, creativity, integrity, money, fitness, and many more. The number of people who participate annually makes Landmark Education one of the largest, most relevant, and most diverse "campuses" in the world.

A fundamental principle of Landmark Education's work is that people and the communities and organizations with which they are engaged have the possibility of not only success, but also fulfillment and greatness. It is to this possibility that Landmark Education and its work are committed.

Find out more about Landmark Education by visiting www.landmarkeducation.com.